MEN
EXPOSED!

A book guaranteed to solve all your problems with guys... even the really dopey ones.

(Written by a certified guy!)

Ben Goode

Published by:
Apricot Press
Box 98
Nephi, Utah
84648

books@apricotpress.com
www.apricotpress.com

ISBN 1-885027-43-5

Illustrated & Designed by David Mecham
Printed in the United States of America

Forward

OK. This book is all about exposing men. "To what," You ask? Not to anything contagious, that's for sure, but hopefully to some A-grade literature and humor. It is expected that this book will also expose lots of secrets about guys to ladies who can doubtless use this information.

We realize that for generations there have been stresses between men and women. I'll bet 6-billion years ago trilobite women were complaining about trilobite men and trying to get them to change. I'm all but certain that even lungfish have been confused about the opposite sex for billions of years; how on earth can they even tell which lungfish is the female?

Of course we know that Adam was certainly confused, as was Eve. Anthony and Cleopatra were also confused, as was Henry the VIII (8) and all the women who lost their heads in that deal. Gender stress has a long history. I'll bet many of you are also confused.

I am a certified man, and as such am in a perfect position to reveal all our guy secrets about which the ladies have always wanted to know. This book guarantees to solve all your problems with men—even the really dopey ones. Yes, if you apply the solutions outlined in this book, your problems will be dwarfed as you wrestle to manage a whole bunch of new problems—and you, of course, will learn from your bad experiences and grow to become a better person as you overcome these new problems, and you will gain perspective. I think that should be good.

Introduction, further forward, or something

I'm sure that to all the guys this book is considered a total cheap shot. Sorry guys—I really need the money. It's true that you would likely never have a woman betray her gender in this way (unless, of course, you include the women's rights crowd), but after all, you've said it yourself, "What's this world coming to?" This book is clearly a symptom of the times in which we live. After all, you have corrupt politicians, rotten schools, corrupt politicians, the destruction of traditional family values, dogs and cats living together, corrupt politicians, and Lady Gaga. Sooner or later somebody was destined to write this book and exploit men and their vulnerabilities and get rich. Well, I'm it.

While I am sure that some guys are going to be upset about being exploited, some will probably be OK with it. Some are used to being exploited; and a lot of ladies will be thrilled. And what could possibly be more useful than thrilling a whole bunch of ladies?

- Ben Goode

Contents

MEN Exposed!

1 How To Communicate With A Man

We all know how important good communication is to the success of any relationship. Some experts have called good communication "the mosquito repellant at the outdoor picnic of life." In our opinion, way too many couples have had their picnic ruined by those old communication mosquitoes, along with symbolically getting the trots from the rancid potato salad of financial stress, or the cold fried chicken of infidelity, or even the mushy watermelon of selfishness. The obvious point here is that some women find trying to talk to men confusing. We believe that all you women who are on the edge of insanity should probably stop trying to talk to men, but for the rest of you, I offer the following: a few keys to understanding what a guy really means:

The Keys to Clearly Comprehending What A Guy Means

Some women seem to get all upset whenever they talk to guys. Because they often don't get the response they anticipated, they assume that he is too dense to understand what they are talking about, or that their guy wasn't listening. This is very unfair. Most likely, the woman is just unaware of the different methods men use to communicate.

It is a well-established fact that women have their subtle ways of communicating, which guys often fail to recognize and properly interpret. It only stands to reason that guys, too, have their codes of communication that most women fail to pick up on. For reasons known only to scientists who study this compost, these uniquely male ways of communication have been rarely studied. Therefore, they have remained secrets from womankind for ions of time.

Here's Where We Get Into Trouble

There is probably nothing in this book that will get me into bigger trouble than what I am about to do, but I think this lack of misunderstanding has gone on entirely too long. Yes, I am about to reveal to you women out there huge secrets about what guys really mean when they communicate in guy code. These are monster secrets, secrets that are so big they make the dump look small when you are about to start combing through it to search for your wife's wedding ring, as big as your Dodge truck looks parked alongside a Subaru. These secrets are so secret it's possible the omniscient creator of the universe may not even be aware of them. And as far as I know these have never been revealed to womankind in the history of the world until right now. What I am about to do may get me labeled a heretic, excommunicated from the male fraternity and kicked out of every sports bar on the planet. It could get me exiled or killed or placed into the witness protection program or forced to be on a demeaning reality game show where I have to eat bugs or something. Oh well. Here goes.

The Secrets of Guy Communication

Guys often communicate in code. They intuitively insert everyday objects into their speech that act as metaphors, which clarify their true meaning. These word pictures help the male mind focus and see very lucidly what meaning was intended. Instead of using vagaries and subtleties, guys wish women would be more forthright and direct and also use these word pictures and metaphors to make their meaning unmistakably clear. The following examples illustrate how guys do this.

Example #1

Let's say you have just finished explaining about your friend, Jennifer's struggles with the subtle digs Amy has been getting off at her lately. You have been describing this with great feeling for 20 minutes, and after your explanation your guy looks up from his sports page and comments: "That's certainly interesting--the Cubs beat the Phillies using five pitchers."

Many women would be hurt or angry hearing this response. They might give their man the silent treatment for days causing both to be in abject misery. This would be totally unnecessary. If she reacted this way it would be because she simply failed to understand his true "guy" communication. In this example, as guys often do, he was using a visual word picture, or metaphor. What he really was saying was: "Honey, I love you very, very, very much, more than all the life bundled up in cute, little fluffy animals like cubs, and phillie's—or even bunnies. And furthermore, yes, your descriptions of Jennifer and Amy's travails was compelling and gripping. I am only holding up this newspaper as a symbolic barrier protecting my tender vulnerabilities, hoping it will symbolically absorb some of the slings and arrows you must be tortured with right now to help me remain composed as I try to deal with your obvious pain so I can give you comfort."

Many women are thrown off because they interpret what guys say literally. You should never do this. Guys speak in a symbolic code; in the example above he used names of sports teams, cute, little animals, and a newspaper to clearly and unmistakably convey meaning. This code makes perfect sense to guys. This is the way they naturally communicate. If you think about it, you will also recognize themes like these that run through all guy communication. If you focus on the objects he's holding or using, and the nouns he uses, this will help you accurately interpret what he REALLY means.

EXAMPLE #2

After his woman takes an hour pouring out her heart to him describing how difficult it is for her to handle his mother's hints that she isn't good enough for mama's little boy; when she finishes, her guy looks up from his computer and quips: "Heh heh, Look at that. I thought John would drop out of our game after I embarrassed him."

Many women would be tempted to be angry and hurt, incorrectly believing that just because he is biologically incapable of doing two things at once, because he was on the computer, he hadn't heard a word she said. Fortunately, you have this book and the secrets that will free you from these erroneous interpretations.

This is obviously a great guy you have here. You are so lucky to have him. He is clearly torn apart in agony for the struggles you are going through with these stresses from his mom. The code word he used was, "embarrassed." He symbolically used the common male name, John, which, as you know can also mean "port-a-potty, a place of comfort he can sneak off to whenever he is in great pain and discomfort, as a metaphor revealing the pain, anguish, and empathy he was feeling for you. What he really meant in guy-speak was, "Dearest, my love is like a river flowing eternally in the same way this computer's electrons flow through the chord, like a river to the sea and you are the kelp and mollusks. My mother can't hold an exoskeleton to you. However, I must use this computer, which is shaped somewhat like an undersea creature, rock, or other formation, in order to deflect some of the pain that you are obviously feeling about my mother, because I am so vulnerable and sensitive that it will tear me apart."

See how easy men's language is! With these keys you are now prepared to properly and consistently interpret your man's true intent. Imagine his pain and frustration if you interpret his response literally and fail to pick up on what he really said! This unnecessary misery has been going on between men and women for millennia, all because of failure to understand one another. What a tragedy!

If I give one more example, I'll bet you can go on from there and interpret accurately the responses of every guy in your life.

Example #3 - Your Turn to Interpret

After she has taken an hour describing how it makes her feel to have to move away from her friends and family to support him in his new job three states away, and another twenty minutes describing how bored and lonely she is without any friends, and how much she would like to do something social with adult companionship, her man looks up from his text-messaging and responds, "I just got invited to go hang out with some of the guys from work tonight. Do you have any problem with that?'

There, now it's your turn. Using these principles of

guy communication we taught you, I'll bet you can interpret what he was really saying. Remember to look very closely at the imagery of the objects he may be holding in his hands.

Random Additional Tips to Use When You Really Need to Communicate with Your Man

As shown above, women often misunderstand men's unique ways of communicating. This may come as a complete surprise but men often misunderstand what women say as well. One of the problems is that the message received and interpreted by the guy is often not the same one intended by the woman in question. In order to help avoid conflict and misunderstanding, I give you the following additional insights into how to properly communicate with your man. You can do this!

Screaming At Your Man

When most women scream at their men, they scream to have them clearly understand the actual words coming from the womens' brains, and flowing out their mouths. While some women appear to scream just because they like to, or because their vocal chords need the exercise, many women want their man to actually interpret the words they are screaming and understand that they mean these words forcefully…in a screaming kind of way…or something like that. However, regardless of the actual words she's using as she screams, what goes through a guys mind when a woman is screaming at him is not what she thinks. It is probably something like this:

MEN Exposed!

What the guy thinks: "This is just like marine boot camp. New marines get screamed at like this all the time. I'm just like a Marine. Marines are super tough, and manly; therefore, I must be super tough, and manly."

It's easy to see that when you convey this particular message by screaming, your guy will begin to behave like a Marine. If you have a wimpy guy and are trying to increase his manly quality, this could be exactly what you're going for. As you can see, properly used, screaming can be a highly effective way to mold, shape, and engineer a better quality guy than the wimpy one you started out with. For some, however, a Marine is not exactly the result they're after. They want to communicate something altogether different. In that case, instead of screaming, YELLING may be the tactic for you. However, you need to understand that things may not go exactly like you think they will when you yell. Women often believe that when they yell at their husband, fiancé, or whomever, his thought process will be something like this:

Her: "You loser, goofball! I can't believe you spent the money we were saving to buy me a new i-Pod on brake pads for my car! What were you thinking?!?"

What she's likely thinking that he's thinking is probably something like:

"She's right. I am a goofball. I should have got a 4th job so we would have had money to buy her i-Pod AND brake pads along with the beach vacation to Jamaica with her girlfriends."

What he's most likely really thinking is something like this:

"Do the Cowboys play the Eagles this Sunday or was it week seven? What's that awful noise?"

Since many women do not always want to convey this particular message, sometimes yelling is not the best thing to do. Fortunately there is an alternative to yelling. You can also communicate through other means. A little scientific background may be helpful here. You need to know the following basic psychological facts. There are some intricate little ear-to-brain parts in guys, which do not occur naturally in women. These develop inside a man's head, which connect the eardrum and the sounds you're making to his guy-brain. These include the anvil, hammer, spatula, cordless drill, blackberry, and joystick. When a woman speaks to a man at a relatively low volume, these all coordinate perfectly to pass along a clear, unmistakable message to the brain, which a guy interprets something like this:

"Hey, she's talking quietly to me. That's certainly romantic. She must be feeling amorous."

If a woman does not want to convey that particular message, she needs to crank the volume up a notch, in which case these little ear-brain parts also coordinate perfectly and convey a message that a man's brain interprets something as follows:

"Hey, she's talking somewhat forcefully to me about this. That's exciting. She must be feeling amorous."

When a woman gets so worked up that she decides

MEN Exposed!

to really crank the volume up but she doesn't want the results she will get from screaming or yelling, it is best for her to use a technique known in scientific circles as "HOLLERING." When she hollers at her man, this is what happens: At a certain volume and intensity, these tiny, delicate inner ear appliances jump the track tripping the brake to the receiving brain hemisphere. They then forward the message to Jerry Springer or some inner city rap group. Since these people will have no idea what she's even talking about, they will most likely add her lyrics to the song they are singing or introduce them as a new wrinkle in the screening of the television show already going on in the studio. The guy being hollered at will therefore be completely unable to comprehend what she is so upset about and will sit there in a total stupor, possibly able only to blink his eyes.

As you can clearly see, thanks to modern day science you now know that in order to have your guy hear and interpret what you actually want him to hear and interpret, you must be careful enough to adjust the volume and tone of your voice so it's at just the right level to convey the precise message you're trying to convey in order to get the exact reaction you want as illustrated above. Good luck! Now go out there and have a wonderful relationship!

Fascinating Factoids About Men: Part 1

☞ Because they generally grow more muscle than women, men have a metabolism that burns more calaries than women while resting. That's why, when compared to women, men are more often seen resting.

☞ As a boy grows into a man, his voice lowers, his body undergoes a growth spurt, fuzzy whiskers begin to appear on is cheeks, and his sense of humor begins to change from one that women often find silly and obnoxious, to one that they usually find silly and obnoxious, but more mature.

☞ The male brain does not intuit the world holistically like most women do. This makes it impossible for most guys to "multi-task." Nature has compensated by giving guys extra sweat glands.

☞ Male ducks and many other male birds have beautiful plumage. Females, on the other hand, are plain. Bummer.

☞ Because men's bodies generally produce much more sweat than women, the bacteria, which grow rapidly on men, often cause the toilet seat to stay up.

☞ The average male apologizes to his wife 37 times-a-day; most of the time for the same thing over and over.

☞ The average male weighs 38 pounds more than the average female. The majority of this extra body mass consists of coarse hair and ego.

MEN Exposed!

One sure-fire way to avoid the financial stresses that so often ruin your relationships

Many of the biggest problems between men and women revolve around money. There just never seems to be enough to go around. Being sensitive to this we have a terrific idea, which can bring you great wealth if we are to believe the celebrities who have launched their careers and made millions this way. While it is probably the guy who will be the one who needs to use this information, nevertheless, we have included it in this book because it is a big secret, and because you ladies may need to encourage your man to follow through and do something like this to solve your financial problems, thereby saving your relationship...and to become rich as stink.

Apologizing Your Way to Fame and Fortune

Yes, even you can apologize your way to fame and fortune. In the process you can get away with fun, cool, and also heinous, despicable, and reprehensible things any time you want...and make a big wad of cash in the process.

It is clear that the rules of engagement in life are changing. A day hardly goes by that some celebrity or famous official doesn't go before the world and apologize for something despicable or reprehensible that he or she was caught doing. As a general rule, they get enormous amounts of celebrity attention that would be impossible to pay for, and then remarkably, they wind up much better off afterwards. There are literally hundreds of celebrities from every walk of life: politicians, actors, sports figures, and authors who have tapped this resource. Not only did their confessions of the grossest misconduct do them no harm, but afterward, their popularity and wealth usually soared. Having studied this phenomenon, I have discovered some of the keys to a good, financially successful Mea culpa.

Some Dispicable and Reprehensible Things to Say and Do Whenever You Need Fame, Profit, or Just Want to Have Fun

First, take responsibility for your behavior. Wait--don't panic. I don't mean you should actually take any responsibility by changing behavior, making restitution or anything like that. What I'm suggesting here is that you take responsibility verbally for your actions. All you really need to do is, while making your public apology; state very clearly without snickering, that you "take full responsibility for your actions." Repeat after me, "I take full responsibility for my actions." (Be careful not to name any specific actions for which you take responsibility, however. This could get you into big trouble later.)

There. See how easy that was! What this simply means is that you take full personal responsibility for some of your actions, the ones you're proud of, or that you're going to spend the next couple of years blaming others for. We are absolutely not talking about the things you're not proud of, or that could cause the victims of your actions to try to get some of your money. You absolutely do not want to take responsibility for any of those actions. If you were to do that, instead of rich and famous, you could wind up groveling for the rest of your life.

Second, be sure and confess to something really outrageous. Nobody cares if you lusted after the Laker's cheerleaders. Pretty much everybody does that. No, to get good fame and fortune from your confession, you have to confess to something truly heinous, shocking and reprehensible, something really out there that the average guy would never dream of doing let alone confessing to. You can confess to just about anything and get away with it now days: infidelity, drug abuse, cheating, murder, theft, adultery, feeding your kids junk food, voting Republican, or hunting deer. The guys who get into the biggest trouble are the ones who did heinous things but refuse to confess. In a study of 1000 Chicago politicians, not only were their confessions not economically harmful to them, but afterward their popularity soared. There's a lesson to be learned here, namely: confessing to horrible things can make you rich and famous.

A Caveat

"What if I have never done anything truly heinous or reprehensible?" You ask. What if I have no disposition to commit horrible acts? What if I'm not a pervert?"

Let's be honest. Some of us are simply not inclined to do heinous and reprehensible things. This is absolutely no problem. You don't necessarily have to do anything despicable to get rich and famous from your mea culpa, you just have to apologize for doing something horrible and shocking. And, of course, take full responsibility for it as described above. Spare yourself the time, effort, and risk of doing something despicable, and simply confess to something heinous that you didn't do and admit it was dishonest and wrong. This act you didn't commit would certainly be wrong in itself but because it's a lie, you are actually telling the truth about having done something reprehensible. Now you are also lying about having done something you didn't do, which is the thing you're confessing to. You have successfully done something truly reprehensible; you've perjured yourself to get rich and famous. Are you following all this? See how easy it can be! These two acts you just committed are acts reprehensible enough to justify a mea culpa that can launch your career in fame and fortune or in national politics, or pro sports and make you rich as stink.

So, if you are someone not inclined to actually do despicable things, you're still set. You can create a legitimate reason for a public apology

Another Caveat

This would probably be a good place to warn you about one other possible danger. Some of you may be considering confessing to having done something reprehensible to animals. Do not do this. For reasons I don't fully understand, now-a-days you can do just about anything you want to your spouse, neighbor, kids, aging parents; you can rape, plunder, lie, steal, murder, just about anything, and with a good, passionate public apology you will get off the hook and probably become rich and famous. But, whatever you do, do not get caught doing anything or confess to doing anything despicable to Sparky or Muffy. This could get you some serious jail time and will likely cost you money.

Another Important Step in Your Success

You must apologize to your fans or constituents. I know, it can be a problem if you have no fans or constituents. Apologizing for something reprehensible may get you some. Blogo was a nobody until he got caught doing reprehensible things. Now you can't get rid of him. Apparently, a good mea culpa will get you fans and constituents and presumably fame and money, along with appearances with Donald Trump.

Some of you would be well advised to confess in advance for things you might someday want to do or that you could conceivably do in the future. In fact, if you can feel your moral resolve begin to slip a little, take preemptive action and confess in advance to whatever horrible thing you are afraid you might not be able to stop yourself from doing. This may get you some fame and money to jump-start your career in fame and fortune before you have actually even done anything deplorable.

Be thorough. This will absolve you of any responsibility should you decide to do something truly reprehensible and will help you avoid the need for restitution...caveat emptor!

Also, it would probably be good for some of you to confess to things you've done but haven't been caught for...see above.

One More Suggestion

You will want to use key props during your public confession. Important props include: your wife. She needs to sit behind you and look very serious. You may need to sedate her so she doesn't break out in sardonic laughter and look heavily medicated on national TV, if you know what I mean. In the event she's not a team player and refuses to appear behind you on TV, you can get a life-sized picture of her and put it behind you. Make sure she looks very solemn. You can get these done at Kinko's for $20.00 these days.

I hope you can see now how easy your path to fame and fortune can be. Take the stress off your relationships with all the money and fame you could ever want. You can still get in on this confession bonanza today, but you may need to hurry. The public could grow weary of dramatic apologies before you get around to yours, and a great opportunity will slide through your grasping and conniving fingers. If you let that happen, you and your sweetie will be stuck with the same kinds of financial problems everyone else has. Don't say I didn't warn you.

Reasons why it's tough to be a guy

☞ It's virtually impossible to get genuine sympathy from other guys.

☞ You are required by law to keep everyone else's cars running.

☞ Even though it's expected that you may smell bad, people will still avoid you.

☞ Even though it's ok to have facial hair, you still have to shave it or wear it and itch.

☞ Without any help at all, even from your dad, you have to figure out all alone how to deal with women's hormone issues.

☞ You have to act like you are tough, even if you're not.

☞ You have to act like you're brave, even if you're not.

MEN Exposed!

☞ You have to act like you've got money, even if you haven't.

☞ You have to act like you are wise, even if you aren't.

☞ You have to protect your kids and wife from lions, bears, monsters, burglars, mice, spiders, telemarketers, etc...

☞ Sometimes you have no choice but to be patient.

☞ Sometimes you really need to scratch, and you can't.

☞ Doctors seem to enjoy doing very demeaning things to you.

☞ If you accidentally run over a cat, everyone will assume you did it on purpose.

☞ Hair will fall out where you want it to grow.

☞ Hair will grow where you want it to fall out.

☞ The women in your life will all remember every thing you ever said or did and keep a permanent mental file.

☞ You have to clean the fish.

☞ You are usually viewed as "The Bank."

☞ You are expected to play football, rodeo, or whatever, even if you are having a bad day, an ingrown toenail, or a headache.

☞ You are expected to be good at video games even if you would rather eat a skunk.

☞ You are expected to always keep the computer running and intuitively know what's wrong.

☞ You are expected to be rational and even-tempered even if you don't feel like being rational and even-tempered.

☞ You can't blame your moodiness on your hormones.

☞ You are expected to be discreet when dinner is awful.

3

Improving Your Defective Guy

Sadly, many of you ladies got into this guy relationship thing believing that making subtle modifications to your guy would be relatively easy. Now that you have been at it a while, you are beginning to understand the magnitude of the project, and so you are overwhelmed and discouraged. Never fear. There are a few tricks that can make your job easier.

A Few Tricks That Can Make Your Job Easier

Let's say you are in possession of a guy who can't tell when his clothes don't match or who otherwise looks like the king of Dweebland in a Halloween costume--

not quite as nice-looking as your 4-year-old who dressed himself. Obviously he is of no value to you in this condition. No one else will take him off your hands, plus it's embarrassing because it reflects on you. People will naturally assume you don't know how to dress your man properly. You are stressing out while your man is running around all over the place looking like a geek reflecting on you. Fortunately, this is one problem you can fix easily.

Usually, all you have to do is complain about how poorly he dresses and speculate out loud what kind of a mother would raise a kid this ill-equipped for life. You will need to do this in the presence of someone who will quickly convey this info to your man's mother...someone like your sister-in-law. Usually, within 24 hours your man will have a new wardrobe and it won't cost you a dime.

Many of you have already recognized there are a couple of potential problems with this approach. First, there will be some of you who actually like your mother-in-law, or for some other reason, don't want to insult her or offend her. And there is also the rare situation where sometimes junior has no taste because Mom has no taste. If either of these situations fits you, don't despair. There are still options.

Without help from his mom, it's tough, but you, like many other women, may have to go it alone. Forbid him to ever leave the house without a thorough inspection. This is what my wife does. This is no reflection on my mom. She dressed me correctly for 23 years—proof was in the fact that I was presentable at the time I persuaded my wife to marry me. Though I had no way of knowing whether my clothes matched or not, they did, which credit goes to my mom. My wife and my mom now have things worked out between them so they have regular, systematic clothing appropriateness inspections because I was diagnosed with an unfortunate severe fashion perception deficiency, or S.F.P.D. If you have a man with S.F. P.D., you may have to enlist the aid of some other strategically placed women, and have constant inspections like my wife does. There will be many women who understand your plight perfectly and will be happy do perform these inspections at work, on the golf course, or in Dweebeland where you spend a good deal of your time etc.

Another Challenge

Fashion isn't the only area of life where men sometimes lack good taste. Another common problem is selecting entertainment. Let's say you get the clothing thing worked out and you decide you want to go to a movie. There is a problem. He wants to go to some lame flick like Terminator Galactica Star Wars Rambo IV, and if you go along you will miss a great chick flick and an opportunity to ogle Hugh Grant and get in touch with your tender feelings. While some guys enjoy getting in touch with their feminine sides, more often, your guy probably has no feminine side, and he will feel threatened and believe that Hugh Grant is really a girl in a wussy guy disguise, and you're going to try to change him or something—so you feel the movie choice slipping from your grasp. You can't allow this to happen. You will need to use subterfuge.

First, having your way will be much easier if you get him his violence fix before you leave home. One easy way to do this is to have him use dynamite or plastic explosives to blow up the clog in the downstairs toilet he has been promising to fix for two weeks. You will need to keep some nitro around for such emergencies.

Second, talk effusively about how romantic Hugh Grant movies make you feel for days afterward. Explain how after you have had a nice meal at Red Lobster, you will most likely be feeling amorous. He'll come around.

Fascinating Factoids About Men: Part 2

☞ When compared to men, women often have better verbal skills. Nature has compensated by giving men chest hair.

☞ On average, women mature four to five times faster than men. They begin to model adult behavior on average, up to seven decades sooner than most men.

☞ Men discovered the steam engine, the computer, a trade route to the Orient, and beer pong. Without men, it stands to reason that we would likely not have any of those things.

☞ It is a hormonal chemical, obstinosterone, which causes the hair on some men's heads to fall out. Women's bodies also produce this chemical, however, when combined with the hormone, estrogen, produced by the women's body, instead of causing her hair to fall out, it often causes money to disappear.

☞ Besides cultural events, which shorten men's life expectancy, such as war, hazardous occupations, gas from bratwurst and sauerkraut, and his inability to recognize when he's too old to climb onto the roof to hang Christmas lights, there are also some biological factors, which also shorten life for men. These include greater body mass, free radicals camping out in the colon and on the west coast, riding in the passenger seat while the wife drives, and stress from trying to understand why women do what they do.

☞ Recent studies have shown that marriage to a woman generally prolongs men's lives and increases overall happiness. On the other hand, the effect of marriage on woman's lives is to prolong the man's life and make him more contented.

☞ Throughout history one of men's top priorities was defending his honor. In more modern times men's main priority is defending the TV remote.

MEN Exposed!

Ben Goode

 **Reasons to Date and Marry a Wimpy guy**

This is not top secret. Many women are aware of this already. Besides the fact that there are not nearly enough real men to go around these days, there are many good reasons to marry a wimpy guy. Here are just a few.

1. He is not likely to drag you to his cave by your hair.

2. With care and a little effort, you can mold him into a tough guy you can manage or control.

3. In his daily conversations with his mom she will likely reinforce many of the things you're having him work on.

4. If you hook up with a tough guy instead, he may be tough enough to make it so that you won't always get what you want.

5. If your wimpy guy becomes too whiny and irritating you can cast him aside like a smelly sock without serious consequences.

6. If you have children with him, unless they mutate, they should be comparatively easy to manage. At least, when compared to the children of a tough guy.

7. Whenever you get bored or feel mean, or need to build up your ego you can tease him until he cries or tattles.

8. He will let you keep your cats…if you want to…unless he's allergic.

9. *He will let you keep your girl-friends.*

10. *He will let your keep your boyfriends. What's he going to do about it?*

11. *You get to choose the movies.*

12. *You will have someone who will share the laundry and mending chores.*

13. *You can go shopping whenever you want.*

14. *He will probably learn to cook pretty good meals.*

15. *He will bring you tools, screws, lug nuts, and a sandwich when you are fixing the car or truck.*

Something to think about.

5 Frequently asked questions and answers about men

Q: What is so cool about fishing?

A: Little boys are naturally attracted to disgusting things: dead birds, worms, bugs, girl's facial hair, etc...and their brains never actually grow up in the way a woman would understand growing up. Fishing is a culturally accepted way, along with other primarily male activities such as cleaning up your kids' vomit, and pumping out the septic tank, to play with the equivalent of worms and fish guts. It really doesn't get any better than this. Besides, where else can men find as big of a money pit as a fishing boat crammed to the rafters with fish techno gear?

MEN Exposed!

Q: Why are men so dense?

A: A long time ago as humans were evolving there were a series of evolutionary events that caused men to evolve to be what they are today. One of these was the epoch suicide event of 10,000 years ago. What happened was that all the guys who were intelligent had full-on brain meltdowns in unison. It happened as they tried to rationally figure out the recently evolved complexities and subtleties of women. Only the dense and clueless survived this huge evolutionary suicide meltdown event known as "The Paleolithic Brain Extinction Epoch of 10,000 BC.

Q: Since I am so hot, why won't he do everything I want him to?

A: I'm sure he noticed how hot you are; he probably just forgot. He is most likely interpreting all the signals you are sending to mean you want him to play video games and eat pizza.

Q: Most of the men in my life are good at repairing computers, cars, toasters, etc... I married this guy thinking that guys just naturally do those things. He does not. Can I take him back and get another one?

A: The real sleepers in life are the guys that were born with defective repair genes. Most compensate by developing superior intelligence, integrity, an unbelievable sense of humor--and they are fantastic lovers. In other words, your diamond in the rough is certainly bound for greatness. I would hang on to him. As you go along you will likely find some other practical uses for him other than fixing things. No, Honey. This is not self-serving.

Q: Why are guys so smelly?

A: Defending women from cave bears and saber-toothed tigers was tough. Natural selection favored the men who smelled really bad. A guy had to smell really, really, really bad to stop a cave bear in its tracks. As bad as some modern guys smell, some experts believe that the male smell has moderated somewhat in the past few thousand years...fortunately.

Q: Why does he always want me to cook meals at home? Why doesn't he just take me to Olive Garden?

A: He has a primal, even guttural need to save up some money to buy you a tennis bracelet, table saw, and a fishing pole.

(Instead of gutteral, I could have used the more trendy, showing-off big vocabulary word, "visceral" here and impressed some of you, since this could be the correct context for the word, "visceral." I chose the word, "guttural" instead because it kind of means sort of the

MEN Exposed!

*same thing plus it comes from the Latin word "gutter"
and it sounded cool.)*

Q: Why do guys like to shoot things and blow things up?

A: Back in the day, men had to kill and skin things in order to survive.   Most men are naturally lazy. Whenever he was blowing something up he intuitively recognized in his subconscious this was a means of killing a whole bunch of food at once thereby saving effort so he could watch football.

Q: He is always doing stupid things. Naturally, I get mad and stop talking to him. Why won't he intuit what I want?

A: Men's radar has evolved to be able to detect wild boar, mastodon, deer, and elk. It is on entirely the wrong frequency to pick up female brain waves. You can have this surgically corrected, but if you do you risk having him start watching soap operas, having hot flashes, and getting into catfights with your friends.

Q: Why don't guys get back?

A: Biologically, guys are missing that part of the brain that enables them to get back with people. In order to compensate, the male brain grew a very large addition, scientists call it the "fragile ego lobe."   What many women have done successfully is figure a way to prompt him to get back and still have him believe it was his idea. Otherwise the "I'm in charge" part of the brain, which wasn't taken in the rib-woman deal, takes over.

Q: My man has decent groveling skills, but he almost never grovels like I want him to. He always wants to kiss and make up after only a small amount of groveling. I may not be ready for romance for decades. What is his problem?

A: Guys and dogs share a common genetic component. You can get mad at your dog and he will forget it in 3 seconds and want to lick your face and soil your carpet.

Q: Why does he dominate the remote?

A: In order to compensate for women's ability to multi-task, men developed the ability to change channels rapidly. Because of the above-mentioned ego mechanism, they stay with things they are good at.

Q: Why doesn't he ask questions when important things come up?

A: Because most men have verbal skills that are pretty much at the 2-3 year-old level, it takes him a very long time to process communication signals coming in. By the time he deciphers the 20-25 different messages that have been communicated to him, the women in the conversation have long since moved on 3 or 4 times and are talking about something totally new. He is now scrambling to figure out what's going on, and there is no way he can form a rational question before the conversation moves on to another topic.

Q: How can I get him to give me more money?

A: Each guy has the capacity to make only so much money. It could be that yours is maxed out. In order to get more money, you have two choices: One, you can go get a job. Only slightly less complicated is option number two, stringing along multiple guys in order to develop their multiple financial capacities.

Q: How can I get him to clean up after himself?

A: Guys have a fundamental need to have their manhood validated. Therefore, this is often the easiest way to get him to do almost anything. He will gladly fight bears and tigers or fight a war in Asia if it validates his manhood. Manipulate him to clean the house with comments like, "I'll bet a big, masculine hunk like you could easily load the washing machine in less than 5-minutes," and then kiss him on the nose.

Q: Why doesn't he want to watch Anne of Green Gables and Dancing With The Stars?

A: When your man was 2 or 3 years-old playing in the sandbox, he had very limited language skills compared to little girls of the same age. His skills were pretty much limited to grunting and crying. Afterwards, since men have a natural communication inhibitor in their brains which keeps them pretty much at that 2 to 3 year-old communication level for life, they struggle with flicks like Anne of Green Gables because there is a lot of talking and very few trucks, explosions, and toy guns. This is confusing to them.

Q: Why do guys live in squalor?

A: This is a natural defense mechanism. Without the squalor, the only odor would be the guy. As you can imagine, if his odor is powerful enough to deter a cave bear, it can make even guys themselves want to hurl. This distinctive odor would keep him awake at night. The cacophony of other odors he has cultivated in his crib is often able to mask the guy smell so he can sleep at night and otherwise function.

Q: Why do guys usually have to have simple things beaten into their heads?

A: Originally, women were formed when God took one of Adam's ribs. Apparently, in the process they took

MEN Exposed!

quite a few other things from Adam, too, things like estrogen, mammary glands, jewelry, fingernail polish, and the parts of the brain that comprehend fashion and relationships, just to name a few. You might as well try to pound these things into his feet or glutes as into his head since he has no body part that is able to comprehend them when you get finished.

Q: If I decide I'm not picking up his boots any more, how long are they likely to sit there in the middle of the floor until he notices and puts them away?

A: There are many architectural digs dating back as far as 20,000 B.C., where old boots, pizza boxes, and dirty underwear have been found fossilizing right in the middle of the living room floor.

Fascinating Factoids About Men: Part 3

☞ Historically, many men have died defending the honor of their women. Throughout history, presumable, many women are grateful.

☞ In many cultures there is a rite of passage ceremony wherein the boy officially becomes a man in the eyes of that culture. In Western culture this occurs when a young man gets his own i-pod.

☞ Despite a rough demeanor, the male species of most animals has a primal need for security. Witness the ostrich burying his head, the male halibut burying himself in the sediment at the bottom of the ocean, toads burrowing into the mud. In the human species this need is manifested by the desire to leave dirty clothes here and there in case he needs to burrow down into them during times of stress or danger.

☞ Male electrical plugs have no male hormones.

☞ Many struggle to recognize the difference between a male and a female cow.

MEN Exposed!

6

Fun Places To Take A Guy You're Embarrassed To Be Seen With

Let's be honest. Time and time again a sharp, intelligent girl falls in love with a basic, garden-variety guy. Time passes. He's not at all what she expected. Or he's not the guy he once was, or for that matter, he's not the guy she expected he once was. In any case, he's a huge disappointment. So now it's, "what was I thinking" time.

So now you're stuck with this guy, complete with his poor social skills, obnoxious sense of humor, gross nose hairs, belly and all. Reality is there are times when you just absolutely have to go out into public with him. Here are some ways thoughtful women all over the world have decided to deal with the times when they have to go out into public with a guy who embarrasses them.

For starters, sometimes she can sneak out and go alone. There will be other times the simplest thing to do is take along a life-sized cardboard picture of someone better looking, or of her guy photo-shopped up a little so he will not embarrass her so much.

Unfortunately there are the other times, the ones when she must go out and she is really stuck with him. More and more savvy women are choosing to hang out in places they are not likely to encounter people who will recognize them, or who will see this clod and talk about him behind their back.

For the times when you just have to go out into public with your man, we recommend you stick to the places where you are not likely to run into people you know, and who's opinions you care about.

Here are some suggestions:

Take him fishing.

Take him hunting.

Your friends aren't likely to see you on top of a mountain and if they do, they likely won't recognize you in camo.

Take him camping.

Take him to the football game.

There are so many other obnoxious, gross-looking guys there looking and behaving just like him, you won't need to be self-conscious.

Move to the country.

My wife and I moved to the country. She goes into town nearly every day and leaves me here doing guy projects.

Stay home and play video games.

You are also not likely to run into your friends at home playing video games in the basement.

Go to the movies.

If you must go to a movie, if you go to a vampire movie or some other touchy-feely one, you'll likely see people there you know and you will need to lie or act weird. On the other hand, if you go to Rambo 27, you can feel safe and relaxed knowing you are not likely to run into anyone you care about.

MEN Exposed!

Ben Goode

7 How To Spoil Your Man

A man is a finely tuned precision machine. If properly maintained he will give you many years of
trouble-free use. Unfortunately, many women do not
take care of their men and thus, through neglect and
abuse, do not get nearly the mileage out of him they
should. The following are a few service tips that will
keep your guy chugging along smoothly and trouble-
free for decades:

Do Not Every Criticize or Nag Your Man.

This will spoil him. When you nag a man, his
natural inclination is to humbly accept your criticism
and suggestions and then to promptly make the recom-

mended changes. This will naturally result in systematically increasing his success ratio in everything he does. He will experience success after success after success until he will be amazing. His being amazing will result in many, many compliments, which will then go to his head. Trust me. I know how guys are. I am one. He will take credit for his success until his ego will become so large he will become insufferable. He will drive you nuts! It is much better to bite your tongue and let him bumble along doing what he thinks is best, and therefore, consistently screwing things up. Between repeatedly screwing things up and your "I-told –you-so's," he will stay humble enough that you will be able to stand to live with him.

Do Consistently Praise and Show Enthusiasm for His Bone-Headed Ideas

Tell him regularly how smart he is. If you do this, he will be more likely to actually carry out his goofy ideas and plans, which will cause him to fall flat on his face over and over again. The repeated failures will keep him humble, meek, and manageable.

Never Interfere with His Hunting, Fishing, or Video Games

These are essential to his growth and development. This constant repetition of participating in manly activities is essential to keeping his sensory and mental facilities sharp. The last thing you want is to be stuck with a man who has bad sensory and mental faculties. Without these he will become dull-witted and indolent. He will lose his cool sense of humor. As he thus loses his ability to function little by little he will become a larger and larger burden to you as he winds down, until ultimately he will cease to function altogether and die.

Do Encourage His Canstant Hunting, Fishing, and Video Games

If he exercises regularly doing these things, the growth and development of his sensory and mental faculties will become so developed that you will have created the most efficient and productive man around. This will make you the envy of master man-developing women everywhere throughout Pakistan and the Middle East.

Do Feed Him Wonderful Meals at Least 4 Times per Day

Poorly fed men become cranky and self-centered. I know some men who were food deprived who could do nothing except sit around and demand food, food, food. Trust me. You do not want a man like this. After you have put all that effort into not nagging him, and after you have encouraged him to hunt, fish, and play video games, and he is humming along like a male Mazeratti, being amazing and efficient with phenomenal sensory and mental faculties, it wouldn't make any sense at all to deprive him of gasoline (metaphorically speaking), or to symbolically put regular gas into a guy who requires nitro or jet fuel. You want to take care of him by feeding him elaborate meals made of prime rib, mashed potatoes and gravy, lobster tail, brisket, and so forth five, six, maybe seven times-a-day to keep him running like the precision fighter-jet you have made him into. Go girl!

How to Keep a Guy Around

While we certainly understand that the problem isn't usually keeping a guy around, the problem is often how to get rid of a guy who is clueless and doesn't get it. Nevertheless, we offer these suggestions just in case you want to keep a guy around and don't know how.

☞ Suggestion number 1: Have a great job and pay for his food, housing, clothes, and car and buy him lots of electronic toys…bag that. Let's not waste our time explaining something that is that obvious.

How to get rid of a guy when you really need to

If you REALLY, REALLY need to get rid of him, do all of these at once.

☞ Leave feminine hygiene products scattered all over the house.

☞ Give him his "honey do" list.

☞ Invite your mother to stay with you for a year.

☞ Tell him that you expect him to join you starting a new diet today—all three meals will be leafy, green salads.

☞ Adopt 20 cats from the animal shelter.

☞ Create 3 or 4 consecutive bad meal experiences for him.

☞ Introduce him to your new boy friend.

☞ Work hard to get in touch with his feelings.

☞ Start making him responsible to pay the rent, buy the groceries, etc...

☞ Constantly, relentlessly compare him to your other lovers.

8

SECTION II:
Making your wimpy man more manly

I'm sure you have noticed, as I have, the acute shortage of truly manly men. The decline in real tough guys that has occurred over the past few years is alarming to social scientists, humor columnists, and real women. Sadly for you women, many of you are either forced to settle for a relationship with a series of gushy wimps throughout your life, or else the only other option open to you is to take on the overwhelming project of trying to make a pigskin out of a silk purse, symbolically, of trying to transform a wussy guy into something of a man.

Until this book, those of you who refuse to settle for something less than a man, have had no help.

MEN Exposed!

You have been completely on your own. Now, finally we have legitimate information that can help you in your quest to turn a mamby-pamby sort-of-a-guy into something really bad; and we mean bad in only the best way.

Only a generation or so ago, men were occupied fighting evil in the world, hunting wild beasts in the forest, watching the Saturday night fights, and refusing to ask directions. Now-a-days you find these same guys, and I use the term "guys" very loosely, often only in a biological sense, doing things like washing dishes, shaving their legs, getting in touch with their feminine self, and suffering through post partum depression. What has become of guys these days?

Years ago, with the birth of our new baby girl, I announced to my wife that I would not be changing any diapers. Now, 30-years and 10,000 diapers later, I realize that I have degenerated into a card-carrying, nose wiping, soap opera-watching wimp. How could this be? I have as many male hormones as any three or four normal guys.

I have been driven, compelled, even slightly interested to answer this question. I have spent countless hours doing exhaustive research, while staring at my eyelids or washing dishes. The only somewhat legitimate answer I can come up with is that it must be some portion of a vast right-wing conspiracy. Whatever the reason, I am fighting back. I am getting reacquainted with my masculine self. I am going to become the insensitive, manly guy I once was. You can too.

These next few chapters in this book will help you try to make a real man out of your husband or boyfriend, too…hopefully

MEN Exposed!

Ben Goode

9 Why Your Wimpy Guy Is Wimpy

It usually comes as a complete surprise to most guys, politicians, and feminists when they finally discover that God made men different from women. And I'm not just talking about their different views of shopping and football, no, there are some fundamental differences between men and women that go clear to the core. For example, nearly all men have a chemical in their bodies produced by the rock and roll rubber gland, which secretes Tabasco Sauce onto their burritos and nachos. Besides causing them to smell bad, this hormone makes them want to jump around and yell, "Yowee!!!" but of course he knows he can't because people would think he's wimpy and can't hold his hot sauce.

MEN Exposed!

Many women's bodies, on the other hand, secrete a chemical known as cacau, which causes chocolate whenever they watch tear-jerking drama or catch up on gossip. This chemical often causes them to want to eat tons upon tons of chocolate mousse cake, Reese' Peanut Butter Cups, and trifle, which of course they know they never could because it would cause all the other women's gossip glands to go haywire and make their thighs the topic of conversation throughout the entire neighborhood and in the tabloids. These are only a couple of thousands of biological differences between men and women that we know of. Most of the differences are as yet unmapped by science, so you can see that there is a lot of work to do in the field.

Most of these biological differences have evolved over eons of time. To begin to understand them, a person must go back billions of years to a time when there were only little blobs of yucky stuff fermenting in rock cracks or "fissures". Going back billions of years like this is very hard to do without a time machine, and so the only thing a good scientist can do is make some plausible sounding explanations up and hope somebody will buy into them so the government will continue his grant money.

A bolt of lightening struck this primordial soup and despite the fact that every junior high biology student knows one of the basic tenets of biology is that all life springs from other life. This principle God apparently chose to suspend just long enough for a disgusting clot of these yuck molecules to come to life.

Two of these freshly living single-celled organisms started to insult each other. "Hey slime ball!" One would say. "Yeah, mucous bag." The other would retort. We could give them the benefit of the doubt since they were in actuality slime balls and may have simply been being blunt and honest or naïve and had no intentions whatever of insulting each other. How should we know? In fact, it's hardly possible that basic social skills had even been invented yet, but since we were not there, we will never know. In any case, the other disgusting single celled organism took it as an insult and started giving it back. Before long they were belching, arguing over meaningless video games, and pulling on one another's fingers.

Meanwhile, the other two or three single-celled organisms felt differently about the insults and pulled fingers and began to act disgusted. They talked among themselves about how disgusting and fashion unconscious these other cells were and how they would die before they ever went out with any of them. However, it soon became clear that there just were no other options since every other mass on the earth was a rock, and so they began to swallow hard and accept a date here and there from these aforementioned slime balls.

Fast-forward a few billion years. Here was Cro Magnon man, hairy, bad smelling, burping. He would brag relentlessly about the mastodon he slew. In meaningless games of rolling the rodent bones, he and his buddies would get so wound up and competitive that often they would crack open each other's skulls with

MEN Exposed!

their saber-tooth tiger femurs, insult each other, and laugh doing it. Cro-Magnon was an extreme guy in every way. He would leave things around the cave in piles without cleaning up. He would shower whenever he wanted to, which was never. He would go hunting with his buddies because he had to, in order to keep from starving. On the other hand, Cro Magnon woman had no choice but to stick with this lout because somebody had to protect her from hungry cave bears, tigers, and sharks. Life for Cro-Magnon woman really stunk...in a very literal sense.

Then, finally came the 1960's, and the various women's movements and lawsuits for sexual harassment. Women didn't want to put up with smelly, violent disgusting guys any more, and thanks to an abundance of aggressive lawyers, they didn't need men to protect them from cave bears anymore. Women began to demand that guys act more like women. Besides expecting them to shop and gossip, they were also expected to shave their chests and legs, to shower regularly, and not shoot things or blow them up. Many guys of excessive testosterone were jailed for sexual harassment when all they did was enter the room. Many politically incorrect men were simply unable to get any women to date them in order to eventually have children.In this way, gradually the gene pool began to shrink. Fewer and fewer real men were left until we are now to the point that we have Pee Wee Herman, Spencer Pratt, Barney Fyffe, Gilligan, Hillary Clinton, the country of France, and the state of California.

Unlike in all former times, today, wussy men are allowed to reproduce.

I don't want to confuse wussiness with groups that choose to do good kind service like Bikers Against Abuse or the Lone Ranger. It actually takes great courage to fight for truth and right against the Taliban, Nazis, Michael Moore, and the Hollywood PC crowd. I also don't mean to suggest there is anything un-manly about going to a chick flick with your wife just as long as you are only doing it to get back into her good graces, and as long as a guy doesn't actually enjoy it. Real men work to stay in touch with their elk-hunting side.

These days a guy's got to do what a guy's got to do. For real men, it would be just fine to be in touch with their feminine side except they don't have one, so they have to do the best they can against all odds. Good luck men; and good luck ladies finding one.

MEN Exposed!

Ben Goode

Tips for men (and women) who would like to become more manly

10

I realize these days manliness is a delicate topic. However, never in my life to this point have I ever backed down from a journalistic challenge. I have written about things that were highly controversial before; in the past I have covered things that were scandalous, bogus, messed up, and seemingly ridiculous, I have even written things that were complete and utter nonsense. I have also written many apologies, retractions, and mea culpas; with so much experience, I figure I am the guy to take on this topic, so work with me here.

There are many situations where a man or woman needs to be more manly; attempting to break through the glass ceiling, climbing the ladder of success,

MEN Exposed!

neutering the cat, gutting and cleaning the moose, taking on a 300 pound pulling lineman, or getting pressure on the QB when the other team is moving the ball down the field in the final minutes of the game. Sadly, until today, there has never been anything written teaching one how to do this. In recent years we have been left with ridiculous role models who don't have a clue. We get advice from people like the Artist formerly known as Prince, first grade teachers, Karate mentors, or Cosmopolitan Magazine. This book is different. Here are instructions from a genuine guy; secrets, which after having revealed; I could be exiled from super bowl parties for XXXVVVIII years or even more. I am bravely forging on taking this enormous risk because frankly I need the money really bad.

5-Tips for Women (or Men) Who Want to be More Manly for Whatever Reason

First, you need to understand; you are going to need to think outside the box. Simply being unattractive alone won't cut it. Growing an awkward amount of facial hair alone won't do it. There are more essential manly virtues that have been forgotten for nearly a generation or something. Here they are.

1: How to wear clothes that don't match. To start with you have to genuinely have no clue. This can be a real problem if you have a clue. If you are someone who has a clue, you need to stop now.
2: Drive the long way or the wrong way to places

just to prove that who is in charge. This can also be a real challenge. Real men know that they always know exactly where they are going and the best way to get there. In order to pull this one off, then, you will need to have a plan before you leave allowing you to drive in a circuitous route to your destination, way out of the way.

3: How to dominate the TV remote: In order to be a real man you must control the remote at all costs. You must also channel-surf relentlessly until your thumb cramps up. I know this will be hard for some of you because you strong, manly men are perfectly secure in your manhood and have nothing to prove, and so you would naturally want to share the remote with your wife or girlfriend. You must resist this urge at all cost if you want to be a true manly man.

4: Act like you hate to shop. You are big enough to pay for everything and you most likely genuinely enjoy watching your wife or girlfriend's face light up when you buy her cool stuff and watching as she paws through every item on every shelf or table in every women's store. You must act as though you are a tight wad. I know this is against your nature, but you can do it. Be a man!

5: Insult everyone, especially other guys.

There you have it. If you can manage these five skills, you can fool almost anyone into believing you're a manly man.

Ben Goode

11

The Downside to Dating and Marrying a Wimpy Guy

There are secrets guys know that women are always trying to discover. In the spirit of full disclosure, here are some of the big, big secrets guys keep among themselves, which women have been conniving to find out since sometime in the middle of the Pleistocene Epoch. There are some definite downsides to dating or marrying a wimpy guy. Here they are:

You will regularly have to clean the sand out of his eyes.

He will want to borrow your pepper spray.

You will have to pick the movies to watch.

If you fail in your efforts to make him a tough guy, you are likely stuck with a wimpy guy because nobody else is likely to want to take him off your hands.

He will most likely breed wimpy offspring.

He may not be willing to share his electric blanket or sweatshirt or silk underwear.

It will be up to you to stare down the angry dogs and get rid of aggressive sales people.

You will have to learn self defense and protect HIM from mean people.

His daily conversation with his mom can take so long it keeps him from doing the dishes and other chores. (One possible solution is to buy him a headset so he can do some of his chores while talking to his mom.)

You may have to listen to him and the kids all whining at once.

His cats may not get along with your dogs.

Some of his tools he will try to bring you will be too big and heavy for him to manage and you will often have to go get them yourself.

You will need to make all his decisions for him.

MEN Exposed!

12 How to tell if you are really tough

The last time you got a big gash in your leg was the time you took on a dozen or so evil ninjas who had swords and stars, and you stitched the wound up yourself using your leather bootlace and a fork.

You drive a Dodge truck or saddle bronc.

Whenever you go to the doctor to have blood drawn, they ask you to sign a

*permission slip so they can use your
blood as steroids for their wimpy
patients.*

*You completely ruin two or three
razors each morning trying to chop
through your wiry stubble.*

*You have stayed on a bull for at least
five seconds.*

*Whenever you can't find a church key
you bite the top off your Mountain
Dew bottle with your teeth.*

Women worship your biceps.

*Men who have heard of you are afraid
to mess with you.*

*If you don't have clean underwear you
cut holes in a burlap bag or tear off a
piece from a roll of attic insulation…or
you go without.*

*Cats stay out of sight when you're
around.*

You are capable of feats of great endurance like crossing the Gobi Desert bare footed, and climbing El Capitan from the ground to the top using only your arms.

You don't comprehend fear.

You don't comprehend fashion.

You don't comprehend quantum physics.

You keep ripping out the sleeves in your shirts doing simple things like brushing our teeth.

A score of 10 or more = John Wayne

A score of 5 to 10 you can use some help, but shouldn't give up just yet. There is still hope.

A score below five means you' re probably a man trapped in a gerbil's body, or in the body of some other random small mammal. If we were to find a way to get you out of that one you might end up a chicken or something, which could be even worse, so we should probably leave well enough alone.

MEN Exposed!

13 How to Tell How Tough You Are

Here is another test to determine how tough you are. A score of 10 or more means you are really tough and may not need to read this book. In fact, if you score higher than 10, you should probably be writing the second edition.

If you score between 5 and 10, you have some potential; while real tough guys most likely laugh at you. However, if you are willing to work hard there is some hope.

If you score below 5, you definitely don't want to be seen hanging around any Marines or NFL football players, and you should probably keep a low profile when you go to the beach.

Indications You are not Very Tough

Instead of hiding under the sofa, your girlfriend's cat climbs onto your lap.

You are more comfortable going to the restroom with someone than going alone.

You do any of the following on purpose even when you are not headed into surgery: paint your toenails, shave your legs, pluck your eyebrows, or shave your chest hairs.

You feel sorry for the steers at the rodeo.

You drive a hybrid economy car.

You have read all the books and seen the entire Twilight movie series.

You wear a Speed-o and you are not an Olympic swimmer.

Your wife or girlfriend usually gets to pick the movie.

You're a big Laker fan.

Your girlfriend has to change your oil because you do not know how.

You are squeamish about hunting.

You don't understand football.

You are an avid animal rights activist.

You like to shop for and try on clothes.

When you participate in a rodeo, you either rope goats or you are royalty.

MEN Exposed!

14 Reasons to be glad you're a guy

You can smell bad if you want to; it's expected.

If your clothes don't match, are inappropriate, or are in poor taste, it's a reflection on your wife or girlfriend, not you.

If you have facial hair, that's OK.

You are not required to remember everyone's birthday.

MEN Exposed!

If you ever do remember someone's birthday, you get bonus points for it.

You can normally never become pregnant.

99% of the animal kingdom will flee from you in terror out of fear and respect.

99% of women will flee from you in terror; probably not out of fear and respect.

There are many products you can use to replace the hair on your head.

You can go to the bathroom alone if you want to.

If you ever go through childbirth, you will do it vicariously.

If you ever go through menopause it will be vicariously.

Eventually, your midlife crisis will end.

Ben Goode

Some pretty attractive women will sometimes feel compassion for you.

You can stop the car almost anywhere and relieve yourself.

With diet and exercise, weight falls off you.

You don't have to pluck your eyebrows or shave your legs.

If you are discreet, you can enjoy ogling beautiful women.

On second thought, better not.

Your house or apartment can look like your house or apartment.

You don't have to eat salads or broiled chicken unless you have been ordered to eat them by some doctor because of a health condition.

Nobody really cares how much you eat.

MEN Exposed!

If you have paid your gambling debts, you don't have to worry about scary and disgusting guys following you home.

You can drive a dirty pickup truck.

You can sit with your legs apart.

You can act like a little kid.

Ben Goode

MEN Exposed!

Alternative Uses for a Squirrelly Guy

For a while, you thought this guy you had found might have some practical uses. He seemed kind of fun. He picked up the tab for dinner. He scared other more obnoxious guys away. So you made a commitment. If you are one who seems to be witnessing this guy's usefulness diminish over time, and there are many of you, as mega-experts in the guy field, we feel it our duty to inform you that guys often do decline in potency and value with time. Some even become completely worthless. But, since you may have so much invested in this guy that you hate to completely lose your investment, or you wonder if you have the energy to start over again with a fresh guy and see all that effort and expense go to waste, we figured that one of the most valuable things we could do would be to find some other possible uses for your particular guy. If you can put him to some other good use, who knows, maybe he'll come around again.

☞ He can sometimes be useful as your automated teller machine—to become your emergency slush fund.

☞ You can push him in front of you or duck behind him in times of stress to deal with grizzly bears, mountain lions, and sales people.

☞ His smell will sometimes keep certain pests away: deer. Coyotes, skunks, your kids' friends etc…

☞ He can sometimes contribute to the household income by giving blood, selling organs, and by selling his guns, golf clubs, and baseball card collection.

☞ He can be good for comic relief. You have to admit; he would sometimes be pretty funny if you weren't so mad at him.

☞ He is a good place to store your left over ice cream and French fries.

☞ If threatened, or otherwise motivated, some guys will do yard work.

☞ He can operate the remote so you don't have to.

☞ Who else can you to find to leave whiskers in the sink?

☞ He can do all kinds of testing such as tracking mud onto your carpet to see if the Scotch Guard really works as advertised.

☞ Who else could you get to use your good sewing scissors to cut a piece of roofing tin or to cut the hide off a javalina?

☞ Who else are you going to get to eat half the cookies you baked for the bake sale before you leave the house?

☞ Who else is going to smash down his side of the bed?

☞ Who else could you get who will make your parents appreciate the old boyfriends you didn't marry?

☞ Who else can you get to go up onto the roof and fix the cooler so it works only a little worse than it did before?

☞ He can make the $100.00 you pay someone else to fix the things he tried to fix seem like nothing to pay.

'The Truth About Life' Humor Books

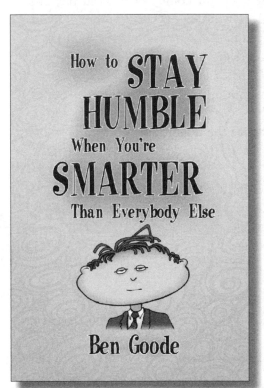

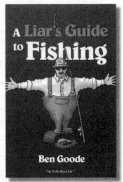

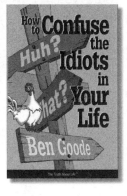

Order Online! www.apricotpress.com

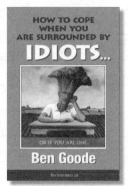

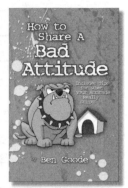

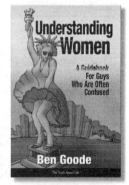

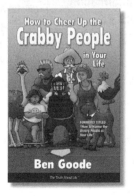

Apricot Press Order Form

Book Title   Quantity x Cost / Book = Total

_____ _____ _____ _____

_____ _____ _____ _____

_____ _____ _____ _____

_____ _____ _____ _____

_____ _____ _____ _____

_____ _____ _____ _____

_____ _____ _____ _____

_____ _____ _____ _____

All Humor Books are $6.95 US.

Do not send Cash. Mail check or money order to:
**Apricot Press   P.O. Box 98
Nephi, Utah   84648**
Telephone 435-623-1929
Allow 3 weeks for delivery.

**Quantity discounts available.
Call us for more information.**
9 a.m. - 5 p.m. MST

Sub Total =

Shipping =   **$2.00**

Tax 8.5% =

Total Amount
Enclosed =

Shipping Address

Name:

Street:

City: State:

Zip Code:

Telephone:

Email: